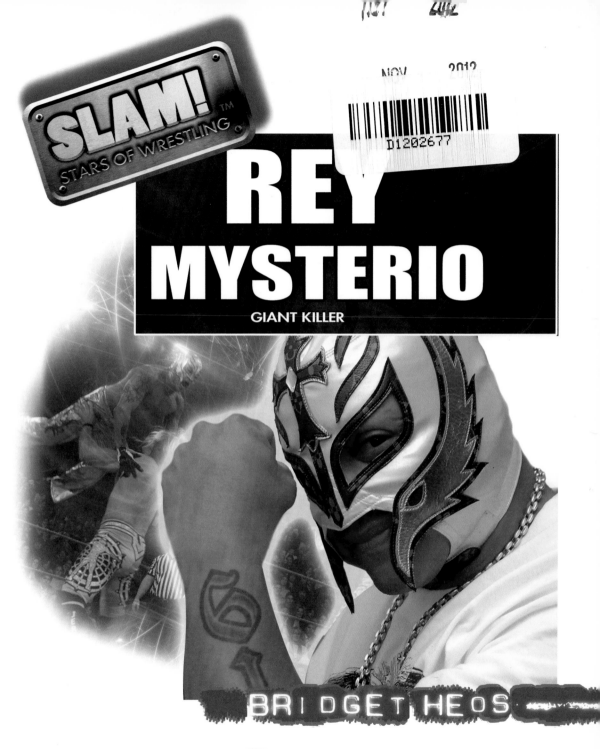

SLAM!™
STARS OF WRESTLING

REY MYSTERIO
GIANT KILLER

BRIDGET HEOS

rosen publishing's
rosen central®

New York

Published in 2012 by The Rosen Publishing Group, Inc.
29 East 21st Street, New York, NY 10010

First Edition

Library of Congress Cataloging-in-Publication Data

Heos, Bridget.
Rey mysterio: giant killer/Bridget Heos.
      p. cm.—(Slam! stars of wrestling)
Includes bibliographical references and index.
ISBN 978-1-4488-5538-4 (library binding)—
ISBN 978-1-4488-5601-5 (pbk.)—
ISBN 978-1-4488-5602-2 (6-pack)
1. Rey Mysterio—Juvenile literature. 2. Wrestlers—United States—Biography—Juvenile literature. I. Title.
GV1196.R45H46 2012
796.812092—dc23
[B]

2011022744

Manufactured in the United States of America

CPSIA Compliance Information: Batch #W12YA: For further information, contact Rosen Publishing, New York, New York, at 1-800-237-9932.

CONTENTS

INTRODUCTION

It was being called a Mexican Death Match. Rey Misterio Jr. was up against a beast of a man: Psicosis. Tall, lean, and wearing a horned mask, Psicosis resembled a rodeo bull. And he was raging like one.

Psicosis climbed onto the top rope. Performing a backward flip—known in wrestling as a moonsault—he landed on Rey. Rey struggled to get up. Back on his feet, Rey was tossed around like a beach ball. Psicosis threw his much smaller opponent onto the ropes.

As it turned out, that was a mistake. When Psicosis climbed atop the rope to prepare yet another attack, Rey held a chair in front of himself like a shield. The tables had turned.

Psicosis tried to run away! Rey chased him through the crowd. He forced Psicosis onto a side stage. Rey climbed atop a platform and leapt onto Psicosis's shoulders, flipping him onto the makeshift mat, in a move called a Frankensteiner. Now, he returned to the ring center. Rey had won the Mexican Death Match. More than that, he had begun the long journey of bringing lucha libre to the forefront of American wrestling. The Extreme Championship Wrestling fans of the late 1990s had cheered the aerial moves and toughness of the Mexican wrestlers, known as luchadors. And they loved that the 5-foot-6 (1.7 meters) Misterio had conquered the 6-foot-tall (1.8 m) Psicosis. Rey's star was rising.

celebrates after defeating John Bradshaw Layfield (JBL) at Wrestlemania V on April 4, 2009, in Houston, Texas. Mysterio (formerly spelled Misterio) quently defeats wrestlers larger than himself.

1 A VERY YOUNG LUCHADOR

Rey Mysterio was born Oscar Gutierrez on December 11, 1974, in Chula Vista, California. His father, Roberto, had been very poor growing up but now ran a factory warehouse in Tijuana, Mexico. Because the family lived in San Diego, Roberto would commute from America to Mexico every day. He would leave at 5:30 AM and return late at night. Oscar's mother, Maria del Rosariao, cleaned houses. Oscar saw his parents' hard work as a sacrifice for him and his brothers.

Oscar had three older brothers: Rojelio, Roberto Jr., and Luis. His uncle, Miguel Angel Lopez Diaz, also lived with the family. By day, Miguel was a construction worker. But on Friday nights in Tijuana, people knew him as Rey Misterio—King of Mystery.

Uncle Rey was a luchador—a professional wrestler in Mexico. The style of wrestling is called *lucha libre*, which means "free wrestling." Like American wrestling, lucha libre is staged but requires great athleticism. It is different from American wrestling in that it is more high flying. Also, many of the luchadors wear masks.

On Friday nights, Oscar would go with his uncle to Tijuana, which they called TJ. Often, his mother and grandmother would go, too. By the early 1980s, Uncle Rey was a well-known wrestler and trainer in Mexico. At 220 pounds (100 kilograms), he was a heavyweight. While Oscar would never grow as big as his uncle, he would surpass him in fame, becoming an in-

Rey grew up as Oscar Gutierrez in Chula Vista, California, a town by the ocean and close to the Mexican border. He would travel to Tijuana to watch his uncle wrestle.

ternationally known luchador. But at age four, he was just a little kid who looked up to his uncle. Rey always made time for little Oscar. He was allowed to watch the big wrestlers at the gym and to imitate their moves in the ring. Backstage, he even got to meet some of the luchadors without their masks—a great honor.

LUCHA LIBRE VS. AMERICAN WRESTLING

Besides masks, high-flying moves set lucha libre apart from American wrestling. While some Americans, such as Kofi Kingston and Ricky the Dragon Steamboat, are famous for their high-flying routines, Americans as a rule are known for their strength moves.

In America, weight class is applied loosely. It's not uncommon for cruiserweights (wrestlers 220 pounds [100 kg] or less) to go up against heavyweights. However, big wrestlers, at least historically, have been more popular. Smaller luchadors, on the other hand, are among the most popular in lucha libre because they tend to be more acrobatic. (In lucha libre, weight classes go all the way down to fly weight, 110 pounds [50 kg].)

Something the two styles have in common is that while they are staged, both require athleticism and risk-taking. Also, both styles of wrestling have good guys and bad guys. In America, they're known as faces (or baby faces) and heels, in Mexico, tecnicos (or cientificos) and rudos. *Cientifico* means "scientist"—or somebody who follows rules. *Rudo* means "a crude person"—one who will cheat or use treachery.

Oscar couldn't wait to become a luchador himself, and at eight years old, he became his uncle's youngest student. The next youngest boy was sixteen! But Oscar's uncle didn't go easy on him. Part of training was to take chops—or punches. When he could take no more, he would walk away. He always returned, though.

The gym itself required a certain toughness from the athletes who trained there. It was old and bare bones. The mat was rough and hardly padded. The rope was a wire covered—only partially—by hose. The ceiling leaked so badly that on rainy days, it actually rained inside. Still, Oscar loved training to be a luchador in his uncle's gym.

The men and boys would exercise for forty-five minutes, practice in the ring for forty-five minutes, and then work out with an individual trainer. The trainers themselves were luchadors. Oscar's included Caballero 2000 (Knight 2000), La Gacela (the Gazelle), and Super Astro (Super Star). Super Astro was a particularly hard teacher. He would make Oscar do five hundred squats and five hundred push-ups at a time!

Like many families, the Gutierrez family commuted between the San Diego area and Tijuana for school, work, and home. When traffic was bad, Rey would walk, as many pedestrians are shown doing here.

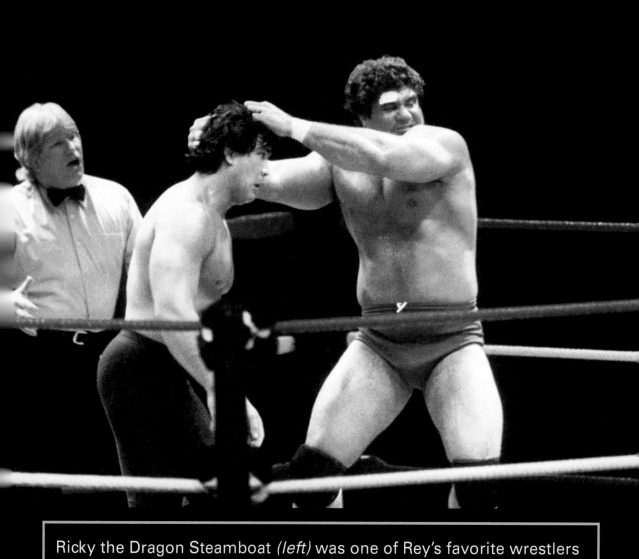

Ricky the Dragon Steamboat *(left)* was one of Rey's favorite wrestlers growing up. Here, he wrestles Don "The Magnificent" Muarco in 1985. He was entered into the WWE Hall of Fame in 2009.

World's Youngest Luchador

After elementary school, Oscar moved with his family to Tijuana so that Roberto could be closer to work. However, the children still went to school in San Diego. Their mother would drive them to school, but when traffic was bad, Oscar would get out of the car and walk several miles to America! Traveling back and forth between Tijuana and San Diego for school, work, and home was not uncommon. Oscar knew many people who did the same thing. Perhaps living between two worlds is what prepared him to merge lucha libre and American-style wrestling later on. This would completely define his style.

In school, Oscar played football at recess. Outside of school, he liked to surf. He and his brothers also had many responsibilities at home. Because their parents worked a lot, the boys had to be independent. By age ten, Oscar was washing his own clothes and cooking his own meals. His specialties were rice and beans, and ramen noodles.

Work is where Oscar first got a taste for American wrestling. In high school, one of his brothers managed a Godfather's Pizza. Oscar worked part-time bussing tables. The TV would often be tuned to a Saturday-morning WWF (now WWE) show. Oscar was impressed by the showmanship of wrestlers like Hulk Hogan, Jake the Snake Roberts, Macho Man Randy Savage, Ricky Steamboat, and Tito Santina.

Oscar also watched CMLL—Consejo Mundial de Lucha Libre (Worldwide Wrestling Council). Based in Mexico City, the promotion featured the biggest luchadors in the country. Oscar hoped to join CMLL someday. And he would. It never occurred to him that he would be part of WWF as well.

Lucha libre has continued to gain popularity outside of Mexico. At this 2010 bout in Bakersfield, California, Mini Kendo watches his tag-team partner, Mysteriosito, jump onto Mascarita Sagrada.

To achieve his dream, Oscar practiced at his uncle's gym from 7:00 to 9:00 PM on Tuesday, Wednesday, and Thursday. Thursday was the best night to practice. The Friday-night luchadors would arrive on Thursdays and visit the gym. Sometimes Oscar was able to get in the ring with big-name luchadors like Negro Casas and Leon Chino.

Oscar often stayed late to practice longer. He didn't mind working hard, but he was getting restless. By age fourteen, he'd been wrestling for six years! He'd seen many classmates turn pro. He wanted a chance in the ring. There was one problem: his size. He was under 5 feet (1.5 m) tall and weighed less than 100 pounds (45 kg). Would anybody take him seriously as a luchador?

2 FEAR THE... HUMMINGBIRD?

Finally, in 1991, Uncle Rey let Oscar take the licensing test. (To wrestle in Mexico, you need a license. This requires a five-hour test, which includes conditioning, moves, and a match.) Oscar was so young that when he passed, it made the newspapers.

Oscar wanted to be Rey Misterio Jr., but his uncle said he wasn't ready yet. Rey Sr. had a green mask on hand, so he declared Oscar the Green Lizard. Oscar didn't like being the Lizard. To make matters worse, his costume was terrible and way too small. Still, he managed to squeeze into it before heading to his first match. Young luchadors like Oscar often start out wrestling at small outdoor venues. Oscar's first match was in a Tijuana churchyard against El Gatonico.

The young luchador continued wrestling in churchyards, on ranches, and at carnivals. Knowing that Oscar was no fan of the Lizard persona, Rey Sr. agreed to change his name—but not to Misterio. Instead, he renamed him Colibri—the Hummingbird. You would think Oscar, conscious of his small stature, would have hated that name. But his uncle had plans for Colibri. He would become a hero to young lucha libre fans. In addition to being named for a small but energetic bird, Oscar began wearing what are known in Mexico as "cake colors." They are the blue, yellow, and red pastels used to frost children's birthday cakes. The plan worked. Oscar got a following among children. They loved that he went up against larger wrestlers and won.

Because of his high-flying moves and other acrobatic stunts, Rey has always been a crowd favorite. Here he performs a splash on Chris Jericho on February 15, 2010.

Even with a strong following, no other promoters (people who put on wrestling events) would consider Oscar because of his size. In training, Oscar had wrestled guys up to 200 pounds (91 kg) heavier than himself. Still, promoters thought he would get hurt. Oscar continued practicing at his uncle's gym, where fellow wrestlers offered him some unusual advice to gain weight. In reality, Oscar was still a scrawny kid. The other wrestlers were grown men. Of course they were bigger than he was!

Finally, Rey Sr. convinced a promoter name Benjamin Mora to put Colibri in an auditorium. Oscar's first arena match was against Shamu (which is also the name of a famous killer whale). Shamu wasn't much taller than Oscar, but he weighed much more. Oscar appeared to be the underdog. However, Oscar's moonsaults (backflips from the top rope, landing on the opponent) got applause. When he finished with a Frankensteiner (in which he straddled Shamu's shoulders and took him down with a backflip, kids were chanting, "Bella lucha! Bella lucha!" ("Good match! Good match!") After a few months, the Hummingbird was being booked for weekend shows. Soon, Oscar was traveling to Tecate and Mexicali for shows.

Oscar's matches were called "popcorn shows" because he would wrestle early in the evening, while people got their popcorn and settled into their seats. Soon, people came early to see the high flyer. Lucha libre is full of high flyers, but Oscar was special. He added twists to the standard high-flying moves to make them his own. He tried to make each match more exciting than the next. Plus, Oscar was wrestling against luchadors he had trained with.

One of them, Psicosis, became Oscar's longtime partner. Standing 6 feet (1.8 m) tall and weighing about 200 pounds (91 kg), Psicosis was much bigger than Oscar. He was also very strong. Together, they invented new moves that showcased Oscar's acrobatic abilities and Psicosis's strength. Oscar trusted Psicosis to catch him when he did a high-flying move. Of course, it didn't look that way. Psicosis made it look like Oscar's moonsaults and Frankensteiners completely blindsided him.

Eventually, Oscar and the his wrestling peers moved with Rey Misterio to a new, nicer gym. A couple of girls a little older than Oscar started hanging around the gym. One was a lucha libre fan. The other, Angie, thought lucha libre was low-brow entertainment. She liked Oscar, though, and wanted to see a match. When she finally did, she loved it. Oscar had a big crush on her. Unfortunately, Angie's mother didn't see a good future for her daughter in dating a luchador. At the time, luchadors tended to be paid poorly. They weren't even offered health insurance to cover injuries. Wrestling had been Oscar's lifetime dream. Giving it up was out of the question.

Then one night, before Oscar's match, the announcer said it was a special night. Uncle Rey came out into the ring. Oscar didn't know what was going on.

Rey would never be a "big guy wrestler." But his athleticism and courage have allowed him to take down giants like the Big Show, whom he faces here, on February 17, 2008, in Las Vegas.

Rey Misterio Jr. Is Born

From the center of the ring, Rey Misterio announced that Oscar was no longer Colibri. And he was no longer Oscar. Now, he was Rey Misterio Jr. Tears filled the young luchador's eyes. He would never be a "big guy wrestler"— even today, he's only 5 foot 6 (1.7 m), 165 pounds (75 kg)—but he was no longer a boy. In the eyes of his uncle and the other luchadors, he was now a man worthy of the Misterio name.

MASCARA

In the early 1900s, lucha libre was brought to Mexico by businessmen who had seen similar events in America. Lucha libre masks, known as mascaras, were used from the beginning. However, they became extremely important to the sport thanks to Santo (The Saint), also known as El Enmascarado de Plata, the silver-masked man. He wore his mask everywhere, including in the many movies he starred in.

Though lucha libre is a modern sport, luchadors see the masks as connections to ancient Aztec and Mayan cultures, in which masks had a religious significance. It's not uncommon for luchadors to wear their masks in public. Some wrestlers won't even take their masks off in the locker room.

Juan Rey and his family make wrestling masks. Because of the hard work and detail that goes into making a mask, the prices can range up to $160.

Matches of great significance are called mask matches. The luchador who loses is forced to unmask, revealing his identity. Even in these matches, the mask is treated with respect by the opponent. The unmasked luchador can continue to wrestle and can later be remasked—often with a new identity.

Soon, a large Mexican promotion would ask him to join its team, but it wouldn't be CMLL, the one he grew up watching on TV. In the early 1990s, some of the CMLL wrestlers and managers broke away from the promotion to form Asistencia Asesoría y Administración (AAA). The new promotion would take a page from American wrestling, which is known for larger-than-life characters, ongoing storylines, and openness to new talent. AAA wanted to spotlight young wrestlers like Rey, Psicosis, and another friend, Konnan. Best of all, the AAA wrestling events would be featured on TV. The young luchadors traveled to Mexico City to seize the opportunity.

Tijuana is more than 1,400 miles (2,300 kilometers) away from Mexico City, or a two-day drive. In terms of wrestling, it was a world away. Though well-known in Tijuana, Rey was an unknown in Mexico City. During his first match, he could tell that the fans liked his high-flying moves.

In Mexico, Rey was becoming more and more well-known. He was also getting a taste of American wrestling. AAA traveled extensively around Mexico and began doing shows in Los Angeles. At the time, some Americans were wrestling for AAA, including Eddie Guerrero, who Rey knew from his earliest days as a wrestler.

At the time, there were two large wrestling corporations in America: WWF and WCW. WWF was Vince McMahon's World Wrestling Federation (now known as WWE, World Wrestling Entertainment). WCW was Ted Turner's World Championship Wrestling. In the fall of 1994, AAA teamed up with WCW for a pay-per-view event called When Worlds Collide. Eric Bischoff, a powerful WCW executive, was supposedly in attendance. Rey and the other luchadors thought the matchup might lead to contracts with WCW, which would mean higher salaries. That didn't happen. However, another American promotion would soon come knocking on Rey's door.

Eddie Guerrero, pictured here on April 3, 2005, grew up in San Antonio, Texas. Rey knew Eddie from his earliest days of wrestling. Several Guerrero family members performed on the lucha libre circuit.

In the 1990s, ECW—Extreme Championship Wrestling—was a new-comer on the American wrestling scene. It wasn't a giant like WCW or WWF, but it had a strong following of diehard wrestling fans. ECW performed no-holds-barred shows in South Philadelphia. In 1995, it added Eddie Guerrero, Chris Jericho, and other cruiserweights to its matches. Soon, Eddie and Chris were recruited to WCW. When they left ECW, Rey and Psicosis took their spots on the roster.

Wrestling for ECW was a bit of a culture shock. In Mexico, wrestling tends to be well-regulated and conservative. Though AAA had adopted some American wrestling characteristics, it still adhered to Mexican rules. The ECW bosses, on the other hand, told Rey that in the ring, there were literally no rules. In addition, a lot of the matches were improvised, getting the wrestlers into a lot of unusual situations.

In 1996, Rey was wrestling in America and well-known in Mexico. But the biggest event in 1996 was his wedding. On May 11, 1996, he married Angie, the girl from the gym in Tijuana. Psicosis was his best man. A few months later, Rey learned that he was going to be a father. Though he enjoyed wrestling for the wild and wooly ECW, he wanted to make a better living to support his growing family. A larger American promotion would provide just that.

3 REY MYSTERIO UNMASKED

Rey's friend from AAA, Konnan, had begun wrestling for WCW. He wanted to bring Rey over, so he began telling management about his friend's wrestling skills. On June 17, 1996, Rey was asked to appear in his first WCW event—a pay-per-view outdoor match against Dean Malenko.

Malenko was a heel known as the Man of a Thousand Holds. He was also the cruiserweight champion. Like Rey, Malenko comes from a wrestling family. Unlike Rey, Malenko was a heel. From his lucha libre days, Rey believed that *tecnicos* and *rudos* (or "faces" and "heels") tended to have similar tendencies in real life. So a rudo would be ornery. Thus, he was intimidated by Malenko, whose other nickname is "Iceman," for his cold demeanor.

Rey was also concerned by Malenko's wrestling style. He was a mat wrestler (hence his nickname, Man of a Thousand Holds). Rey was a high flyer. How would they be able to work together? The stakes were high. Rey was sharing the stage with the likes of Hulk Hogan and Ric Flair. He had seen them in the locker room moments before. He knew that except to wrestling fans familiar with the ECW roster, he was an unknown. Many people in the stands didn't even know what a luchador was. Needless to say, Rey's adrenaline was pumping when he entered the ring.

Rey needn't have worried about one thing: Malenko had experience with high flyers; he had wrestled with luchadors in Japan. This meant that Malenko knew how to use Rey's high-flying abilities to his own advantage. At one point,

Booker T. Huffman shows "Man of a Thousand Holds" Dean Malenko who's boss in this 1998 WCW match. Malenko's long career as a heel prepared him well to work with high-flier Rey Mysterio.

Rey climbed onto the corner rope, and Malenko climbed up there with him. Malenko picked Rey up and leapt off the rope, tossing Rey midair and catching him over his knee. The announcer called it "a gut buster from the heavens." Rey didn't give up, and the announcers noted how much energy and heart he had. When the two wrestlers skirmished between the ropes, Rey caught a break. Malenko lost his grip and fell to the ground. Rey climbed to the highest rope and leaped. But he missed Malenko and landed hard.

Malenko used Rey's moment of weakness to pin him—twice. But Malenko's hubris got the best of him. Malenko thought he could toy with Rey, like a cat with a mouse. Each time he pinned him, he let Rey get up. Finally, he had Rey upside-down by the ankles. He was going to flip him. Instead, Rey flipped Malenko—and pinned him. Rey was the new cruiserweight champion. Not only did Rey and Malenko get a standing ovation from the crowd, they got one backstage from the other wrestlers, too. In wrestling, that means a lot. Especially when the other wrestlers are legends like Hogan and Flair. Not surprisingly, Rey was offered a contract with WCW.

The contract was for less than $100,000—perhaps less than you would think a pro wrestler would get paid. But Rey also got health coverage, an important benefit for wrestlers, who tend to suffer repeat injuries as time goes on. To make extra money, Rey simultaneously worked with Promo Azteca in Mexico. This was an extreme wrestling promotion along the lines of ECW. Eventually, WCW said that Rey couldn't work for both.

By now, Rey Misterio Jr. was Rey Mysterio. Whether because of a typo or in order to Americanize the spelling, WCW had changed Rey's last name. The "Junior" was also dropped. Many Americans weren't familiar with Mexican lucha libre rosters, so they wouldn't know why Rey was called "Junior." Luckily, Rey's new job didn't cut him off completely from his past. One of

REY'S COSTUMES AND SYMBOLS

Rey Mysterio believes wrestlers' personas reflect who they are in real life. He himself is religious, which is why he prefers to be a good guy— a tecnico. His costumes and tattoos include many religious symbols. His masks often include a cross or skull. In Mexico, skulls symbolize life after death. He used to wear a rosary to every match. Once, he forgot it. Afterward, he had a rosary tattooed on his chest so that he would never again have to go without it.

his best friends in WCW was the luchador Eddie Guerrero, whom Rey had wrestled with in AAA. Eddie would play a significant role in Rey's personal and professional life.

On April 5, 1997, Rey and Angie had a son, Dominik. Soon after, Rey tore his ACL during a match with his nemesis, Dean Malenko. (In real life, Rey said that Malenko couldn't be nicer, but as wrestlers, the two feuded.) The Frankensteiner that Rey frequently performed (which he calls the West Coast Pop) had caught up with him. For years, he'd been landing on his left knee. Now, the knee required major surgery. Though happy to spend time at home with his new son, he worried that he would lose his spot on the WCW roster.

After recovering, Rey was welcomed back, but by now there were rumblings among his fellow wrestlers. They thought the Mexican wrestlers and cruiserweights were being treated like second-class citizens. They thought they faced stricter rules from management and didn't get storylines, even if they were popular. Eddie Guerrero decided to create his own storyline,

Latino World Order. Rey played the role of the last Latino holdout. But when Eddie was in a car accident in real life, LWO fell apart.

Rey began being paired with bigger guys. He became known as the Giant Killer. It was good to earn a nickname like that. But Rey was hearing rumors he didn't like. He learned that management planned to have him unmasked. In Mexico, being unmasked is an honorable thing. It shows that the luchador is willing to sacrifice himself for the sport. But Rey thought that in America, the significance of the mask would be lost in the scriptwriting. He worried that the mask would be treated with disrespect. He also didn't believe the time was right to be unmasked. Management backed down from the idea the first time. But soon, there was talk again of Rey being unmasked. Management thought Rey was a good-looking guy. They wanted him to show his face.

The night of the unmasking, Rey and Konnan were in a tag-team battle with Kevin Nash and Scott Hall. Rey and Konnan lost, and Rey was forced to unmask. Konnan helped him. He knew that Rey's sadness over losing his mask wasn't just a show. Rey had been expecting it, but that did little to soften the blow.

When Rey left the ring, Nash put the mask on as a joke. That was exactly why Rey didn't want to be unmasked in America. In Mexico, the mask of an opponent would never be treated disrespectfully. But in America, it was seen as just another prop. Today, Rey wishes he would have fought to keep his mask. It was part of who he was. For him, the fact that WCW wanted him to lose it showed that the organization didn't want Rey to be himself.

In 2002, the situation for WCW Mexican wrestlers and other cruiserweights came to a head. Eddie, Chris Benoit, Chris Jericho, and Dean Malenko left for WWE. Rey, in the middle of his contract, stayed. But even for Rey, everything was about to change. WCW was sold to WWE.

Rey: Remasked

Rey was unsure of his future in wrestling. With a daughter, Aalyah, born August 20, 2001, Rey went home to spend time with his family and to wait for his contract to expire. He also did some wrestling for CMLL—but without his mask. He thought he would like to wrestle for WWE but had heard it only wanted big guys. Then in April of 2002, he got the call.

Jim Ross, nicknamed JR, is a well-known announcer who often sits alongside announcer Jerry Lawler. He wears a suit and cowboy hat. He is also head of talent for WWE. He was eager to recruit Rey to the world's biggest wrestling promotion.

To get used to WWE's larger rings (20 feet by 20 feet, [6 m by 6 m]), Rey wrestled for Ohio Valley Wrestling for a couple weeks. At the time, it was a training ground for WWE wrestlers. There, he met two future stars of wrestling: John Cena (then known as the Prototype)

Jim Ross (JR) is a well-known announcer for WWE and plays a large role backstage. He played a big part in Rey's career, too, recruiting him to the world's biggest wrestling promotion.

and Randy Orton. Rey was still wrestling without his mask. After his very first match, the head of Ohio Valley Wrestling asked Rey where it was. Vince McMahon had specifically asked that Rey wear his mask. That was Rey's first indication that WWE was going to let him be himself: a masked luchador.

After just one week at Ohio Valley Wrestling, on July 25, 2002, Rey was booked in a house show in Los Angeles opposite Chavo Guerrero (Eddie Guerrero's nephew). This time, the announcers knew the history of the mask. They said that it was considered sacred, a superhero-like alter ego. (In fact, Rey's costume that night was inspired by Spider-Man.) Chavo targeted Rey's injured knee, but Rey fired back with a corkscrew dive from the ropes. He finished Chavo with a 619 (in which Rey held onto the top and middle rope and swung his legs through the ropes, knocking down the opponent). It was a great entry into WWE. But soon after, he needed another knee surgery.

Once he had recovered, Rey started a longtime feud with

Chavo's uncle Eddie (a heel that people liked, also known as a tweener). Eddie came up with an angle that involved Rey's son, Dominik, who was now school age. Rey and Eddie asked Dominik if he would like to be part of the drama. Dominik agreed, and the story began. During a match between Eddie and Rey, Eddie announced that he had a secret that would tear Rey's family apart. As time passed, viewers heard a fabricated rumor that Dominik's birth father was Eddie. Unable to care for the boy, Eddie had asked Rey and Angie to adopt him. Rey kept reminding Dominik that this was all pretend, especially when it culminated in a match to determine who got custody of Dominik.

The final showdown was a ladder match. Usually, a briefcase in a ladder match is filled with money. This time it contained something priceless: Dominik's custody papers. It was a brutal match, with the ladders used as weapons. Rey nearly reached the top but got pushed off. Next, Eddie pinned him under the ladder and began climbing. As he reached for the briefcase, he was poised to tear Rey's family apart. Then, out of nowhere, Eddie's wife, Vickie Guerrero, ran into the ring. "Don't do it," she told him. Eddie told her to go home. That's when she pushed the ladder, causing Eddie to crash onto the floor. Rey managed to set up his own ladder and climb to the top. Eddie tried to climb up after Rey, but Vickie wrestled him to the floor. Rey got the briefcase. Dominik was still his, and satisfied fans got their show.

Soon after the feud, Rey got a shocking phone call. Eddie, who was supposed to travel to an out-of-town match, had died of a heart attack. Rey was devastated by this news. In real life, Eddie was a good friend. Still grief-stricken, Rey set his sights on the 2006 Heavyweight Championship.

4 THE HEAVYWEIGHT BELT AND NEW ENEMIES

At Royal Rumble in 2006, Rey competed for a chance to battle Kurt Angle at WrestleMania 22. The winner of that match would be heavyweight champion. Rey entered Royal Rumble as the second contender, a disadvantage, as he had to compete against twenty-eight newcomers who entered the ring. He and Randy Orton, the thirteenth entrant, were the last men standing. Rey defeated him and set a record for longest time in the ring at the Royal Rumble: sixty-two minutes. He would now wrestle Angle for the heavyweight title!

Afterward, he dedicated his victory to Eddie. Then he said that Eddie was laughing in heaven. As a friendly joke, he must have arranged for Rey to be the second contender so that he would have to battle longer. Orton came into the ring and interrupted him. He told Rey he was mistaken. Eddie wasn't laughing with Rey. He was laughing at him. Rey went after Orton, defending his friend. But Orton had already challenged Rey to defend his shot at the Heavyweight Championship belt. WWE manager Theodore Long declared WrestleMania XXII to be a three-way championship between Rey, Orton, and Angle. Rey's chance at the Heavyweight Championship had just gotten slimmer.

Rey, Orton, and Angle performed before a wild crowd of seventeen thousand in Chicago. At first, Angle dominated both Rey and Orton. The crowd vacillated between Rey and Angle. (Of course, no one cheered for Orton, after what he said about Eddie Guerrera.) They chanted, "619, 619" and then "Angle, Angle." It appeared that Angle would prevail. He lifted Rey over his head and threw him, but Rey caught Angle's arm and flipped him out of the ring. Finally, Rey delivered the 619, followed by West Coast Pop, and pinned him. A new heavyweight champion was announced: Rey Mysterio! His family cheered from the front row. Chavo and Vickie Guerrero came onto the stage to congratulate him. However, the pair would soon become his nemeses.

That summer, at SummerSlam, Rey and Chavo feuded over who should carry on Eddie's legacy. Rey and Eddie were like blood. But Eddie and Chavo really were blood. As cousins, they had grown up wrestling together. They had also shared the lying, stealing, and cheating heel mentality. Rey, on the other hand, was a good guy. As Rey and Chavo battled in the ring, Vickie came out to beg them to stop fighting. When Rey climbed to the top rope, she tried to climb up to talk sense into him. Instead, she caused him to fall. Chavo won the match. Soon after, Rey suffered another knee injury. On camera, the knee surgery was blamed on a cheap shot from Chavo.

The feud was all in fun. But in real life, Rey's injuries had taken their toll. Between the knee injuries and a biceps surgery that went badly, Rey had been taking prescription pain medication. Though the medication had originally been prescribed by doctors, Rey now realized that he was addicted. He went to rehab for thirty days. His WWE boss, Vince McMahon, was supportive, and Rey returned to work. However, he was subsequently suspended for violation of WWE's Wellness Code for use of pain medication. Rey said that he had a prescription for the medication due to new injuries, but wasn't given enough time to prove it.

Rey's use of pain medication points to a hard fact about wrestling. When athletes are injured, they are prescribed pain medication to manage pain. Returning to wrestling, the athlete risks reinjury. That leads to further use of

The snakelike Randy Orton, shown here battling Kane on August 4, 2006, in Sydney, Australia, was one of Rey's opponents for the Heavyweight Championship at WrestleMania XXII. The other was Kurt Angle.

pain medication. (And of course, the injury itself leads to pain.) People frequently speak of wrestling as being "fake." But if you watch carefully, you'll see that the moves really can be both dangerous and painful.

No Rest for the Feuding

During a cage match, Rey defeated his onetime friend Batista. As winner, his reward—if you could call it that—was to face wrestling's biggest monster heel, the Undertaker, at Royal Rumble 2010.

That night, as Rey took off his rosary, the lights went out. The 7-foot-tall (2.1 m), 300-pound (136 kg) Undertaker—with eyes pure white—approached the ring. Sinister music filled the air. And when the match began, things only got worse. Because of the height difference, Rey's flip moves, such as West Coast Pop, didn't work on the Undertaker. Rey didn't have the leverage he needed. Likewise, because of the Undertaker's seemingly superhuman ability to recover, Rey's high-flying tackles worked only temporarily. In the end, the Undertaker won.

Another feud put Rey at odds with Albert del Rio, a new wrestler. Del Rio, a Mexican aristocrat, proved to be a good foil to Rey's hard-working common man. Fans loved to hate the way Del Rio called Rey a peasant and made fun of his size.

Perhaps his next feud would prove to be the most dangerous of all. Once again, Rey's mask would be on the line. Dashing Cody Rhodes was a vein upstart and son of wrestling Hall of Famer Dusty Rhodes. Cody was so full of himself that he would insult his fans' appearance and give them "grooming lessons" on how to properly brush their teeth, for instance, before his matches. The man in love with his own face proved an interesting rival to a man who conceals his with a mask.

The Undertaker, pictured here on May 9, 2010, in Monterrey, Mexico, is known as a monster heel. Monster heels are evil and have supernatural abilities to deliver and withstand pain.

During one of their first matches, Rey, who was wearing a knee brace, accidentally broke Rhodes' nose during a kick move. Rhodes was infuriated and accused Rey of doing it on purpose. Because his looks were so important to him, he conducted interviews with his back turned to the camera so that fans wouldn't see his disfigured face. Rhodes underwent reconstructive surgery and returned with a special clear mask to protect his face.

At WrestleMania XXVII on April 3, 2011, in Atlanta, Rey attempts to "unmask" Cody Rhodes, who is wearing a plastic mask after reconstructive surgery. Rhodes had ripped off Rey's mask at an earlier event.

Rhodes had made such a fuss about his appearance that his father, Dusty, came into the ring to scold him. Unlike Cody, Dusty had been a no-nonsense wrestler, more interested in wins than personal appearance. He apologized to Rey for his son's dishonorable behavior and asked Cody to do the same. As it turned it out, it was all a trick! After the apology, Dusty shook Rey's hand—and wouldn't let go. That gave Cody time to attack Rey. Outside the ring, he even unmasked him. This time, Rey managed to protect his face from being seen. But in an official WWE interview, Cody vowed to unmask Rey again at WrestleMania XXVII.

At WrestleMania, the feud culminated with Rhodes removing Rey's knee brace and Rey removing Rhodes's face mask. But when the referee turned his back to set aside Rhodes's mask, Rhodes attacked Rey with Rey's own brace. He won the match. This was an example of the new generation taking their place in the WWE establishment. Rey, though just over thirty-five years old, was a veteran. He had been wrestling for more than two decades, and his body had been through a lot.

However, his legacy is far from over. Rey has come back from surgery after surgery to show his athleticism and determination. He has also

MYSTERIO'S SIGNATURE MOVES

Rey Mysterio's moves are named for his San Diego and Tijuana heritage. They are:

The 619. When the opponent is on the ropes, Rey holds onto the top and middle rope and swings his legs between the ropes, kicking the opponent. This finishing move is named for Rey's San Diego area code.

West Coast Pop. This move is known in wrestling as a springboard Frankensteiner. Rey bounces off the top rope and onto the opponent's shoulders. He then does a backflip, taking his opponent down.

Droppin' da Dime. Rey stands on the apron (the part of the ring outside the ropes), leaps over the ropes, and kicks the opponent. "Droppin' da Dime" refers to making a call on a pay phone, which used to cost a dime. It is slang for calling the police.

Wearing a Captain America–inspired costume, Rey delivers the 619 at WrestleMania XXVII against Cody Rhodes. Professional wrestlers are known for their unique (and sometimes dangerous) moves.

proven to be a likeable guy among fans young and old. In late April of 2011, Rey was drafted to Raw, joining the Big Show, Alberto del Rio, and John Cena. A new WWE luchador, Sin Cara, who made his debut on *Raw*, seemed a possible opponent. (*Sin Cara*, which means "faceless," was a top CMLL luchador for several years before being recruited by WWE.) However, Sin Cara was drafted to *SmackDown* the same night.

When Rey does retire, he hopes to pass on the family luchador tradition to Dominik. Rey, like many pro wrestlers, often brings his children on the road with him. He hopes that Dominik will like what he sees and want to be a wrestler like his dad. Perhaps they will build a legacy along the lines of the Guerrero family. Whatever the future holds, Rey has already changed the face of American pro wrestling. He has shared lucha libre with millions of WWE fans worldwide, opening the door for luchadors like Sin Cara. Many children now wear the luchador masks to events. For them, it's a symbol of a little guy being able to defeat big guys through hard work and creativity. It's a symbol of Colibri—the Hummingbird.

TIMELINE

1920s Once a boxing-like competition, pro wrestling in America becomes a scripted sport.

1929 Inspired by the colorful world of American wrestling, businessman Salvador Lutteroth Gonzalez starts a promotion in Mexico.

1933 With Francisco Ahumada, Gonzalez founds Empresa Mexicana de Lucha Libre, now Consejo Mundial de Lucha Libre (CMLL), the longest-running wrestling promotion in the world.

1942 Santo, a luchador, movie star, and national hero, popularizes the lucha libre masks, or mascaras.

1974 Oscar Gutierrez is born in Chula Vista, Calif.

1980s Oscar's uncle, the luchador Rey Misterio, begins training Oscar at his gym.

1991 Oscar takes his wrestling licensing test in Mexico. He debuts as the Green Lizard.

Early 1990s Some CMLL wrestlers and managers break away from the promotion to form Asistencia Asesoria y Administracion (AAA). Oscar, now known as Rey Misterio Jr., and his friends join the promotion.

1994 Rey joins Extreme Championship Wrestling (ECW) in Philadelphia.

1996 Rey marries his childhood sweetheart, Angie.

1997 Rey and Angie have a son, Dominik. Rey joins World Championship Wrestling (WCW).

2002 WWE purchases WCW and drafts Rey. Rey is remasked, having been forced to lose the mask during his time at WCW.

2005 Rey's good friend Eddie Guerrero dies.

2006 Rey wins the Heavyweight Championship belt.

2008 Rey puts his mask on the line against Kane (the Undertaker's brother). Kane is disqualified. Rey later defeats him at No Holds Barred.

2009 Rey is drafted to *SmackDown*, where he remains for two years.

2010 Rey feuds with monster heel the Undertaker, who defeats the luchador at Royal Rumble.

2011 A new luchador, Sin Cara, joins *SmackDown*. Rey is drafted to *Raw*.

2011 A feud between Cody Rhodes and Rey results in Rey losing his mask. However, he manages to cover his face to protect his identity. It is not an official unmasking.

GLOSSARY

AAA Asistencia Asesoría y Administración, a Mexican wrestling promotion founded by former CMLL wrestlers and managers.

apron The area of the wrestling ring that is outside the ropes.

CMLL Consejo Mundial de Lucha Libre, the largest and oldest wrestling promotion in Mexico.

ECW Extreme Championship Wrestling, a former WWE brand.

face A good guy in wrestling, short for "baby face."

Frankensteiner A move in which a wrestler jumps on an opponent's shoulders and flips backward, bringing the opponent down.

heel A bad guy in wrestling.

high flyer A wrestler capable of doing aerial moves.

kick out The act of raising one's legs to avoid a pin.

luchador A Mexican wrestler or a wrestler who follows the Mexican wrestling tradition.

lucha libre The entertainment sport of professional wrestling in Mexico. It literally means "free wrestling."

pin The act of holding another wrestler down for a set amount of time; in pro wrestling, usually three seconds.

promotion A company of wrestlers that stages events.

rudo A heel in lucha libre.

tecnico A face in lucha libre.

Tijuana A town in Mexico close to the U.S. border.

wrestle The act of physically trying to pin another person. There is competitive wrestling and staged wrestling.

WWE World Wrestling Entertainment, an international wrestling promotion.

Canadian Wrestling Federation

P.O. Box 51004

Winnipeg, MB R2X 3B0

Canada

(204) 988-4986

Web site: http://www.cwfwrestling.com

The Canadian Wrestling Federation is a family-oriented, all-aboriginal professional wrestling promotion.

Ohio Valley Wrestling and Training

4400 Shepherdsville Road

Louisville, KY 40218

Web site: http://www.ovwrestling.com

Ohio Valley Wrestling and Training is an independent wrestling promotion and school where many wrestlers get their start.

Revolution

831 South 5th Street

San Jose, CA 95112

Web site: http://www.prowrestling-revolution.com

Revolution is a California promotion that trains and books luchadors and other wrestlers.

Total Nonstop Action Wrestling (TNA)

209 10th Avenue South, Suite 302

Nashville, TN 37203

Web site: http://www.tnawrestling.com

Total Nonstop Action Wrestling is a national promotion televised on Spike TV.

World Wrestling Entertainment

1241 East Main Street

FOR MORE INFORMATION

Stamford, CT 06902

(203) 352-8600

Web site: http://www.wwe.com

WWE is a wrestling promotion televised throughout the world.

Wrestlemania Reading Challenge

YALSA

50 E. Huron Street

Chicago, IL 60611

Web site: http://www.ala.org/ala/mgrps/divs/yalsa/teenreading/
wrmc/wrmc.cfm

The WrestleMania Reading Challenge is a quiz contest through which kids
can win tickets to WrestleMania.

Wrestling Lutte Canada

7-5370 Canotek Road

Ottawa, ON K1J 9E6

Canada

(613) 748-5686

Web site: http://www.wrestling.ca

Wrestling Lutte Canada is an organization for Canadian Olympic-style wrestling.

Web Sites

Due to the changing nature of Internet links, Rosen Publishing has
developed an online list of Web sites related to the subject of this book.
This site is updated regularly. Please use this link to access the list:

http://www.rosenlinks.com/slam/rm

Black, Jake. *The Ultimate Guide to WWE*. New York, NY: Grosset & Dunlap, 2011.

Garza, Xavier. *Lucha Libre: The Man in the Silver Mask*. Trans. by Luis Humberto Crosthwaite. El Paso, TX: Cinco Puntos, 2007.

Kaelberer, Angie Peterson. *The Fabulous, Freaky, Unusual History of Pro Wrestling* (Unusual Histories). Mankato, MN: Capstone, 2010.

Madigan, Dan. *Mondo Lucha a Go-Go: The Bizarre and Honorable World of Mexican Wrestling*. New York, NY: Rayo, 2007.

Martino, Alfred. *Pinned*. Boston, MA: Harcourt, 2005.

Monsivai, Carlos, Alfonso Morales, Lourdes Grobet, and Carlos Rodriguez. *Lourdes Grobet: Lucha Libre*. Uraguay: D.A.P./Trilce, 2008.

Sweeney, Joyce. *Headlock*. New York, NY: Henry Holt, 2006.

Venville, Malcolm. *Lucha Loco*. Pasadena, CA: Ammo, 2007.

West, Tracey. *Rey Mysterio: Giant Slayer*. New York, NY: Grosset & Dunlap, 2011.

FOR FURTHER READING

Beekman, Scott. *Ringside: A History of Professional Wrestling in America*. Westport, CT: Greenwood Publishers, 2006.

Madigan, Dan. *Mondo Lucha a Go-Go: The Bizarre and Honorable World of Wild Mexican Wrestling*. New York, NY: Rayo, 2007.

Rey Mysterio and Jeremy Roberts. *Behind the Mask*. New York, NY: World Wrestling Entertainment, 2009.

Shields, Brian, and Kevin Sullivan. *W Encyclopedia: The Definitive Guide to World Wrestling Entertainment*. Indianapolis, IN: DK/Brady Games, 2009.

Williams, Jonathon. "WWE: Cody Rhodes Vows to Unmask Rey Mysterio." *Creative Loafing Atlanta*, Retrieved April 11, 2011 (http://clatl.com/atlanta/wwe-cody-rhodes-vows-to-unmask-rey-mysterio/Content?oid=3001733).

WWE.com. "Rey Mysterio." Retrieved April 11, 2011 (http://www.wwe.com/superstars/raw/reymysterio).

BIBLIOGRAPHY

About the Author

Bridget Heos is the author of several books for children and teens. She lives in Kansas City, Missouri, with her husband and three sons.

Photo Credits

Cover, p. 1 Theo Wargo/WireImage/Getty Images; cover (background photo), p. 1 (background photo) Steve Grayson/WireImage/Getty Images; pp. 4–5, pp. 28–29 (ladders)Bob Levey/WireImage/Getty Images; p. 7 © Richard Cummins/SuperStock; p. 9 David McNew/Getty Images; p. 10 B. Bennett/Getty Images; pp. 12, 18 Zuma Press/Icon SMI; pp. 14–15 © La Nacion/GDA/Zumapress.com; p. 17 Denise Truscello/WireImage/ Getty Images; pp. 20, 27 J. Shearer/WireImage/Getty Images; pp. 23, 38 © AP Images; pp. 29 (briefcase), 36–37 Matt Roberts/Zuma Press/Icon SMI; p. 33 Don Arnold/ WireImage/ Getty Images; p. 35 Jam Media/LatinContent/Getty Images; cover background graphic, chapter openers background graphic, interior graphic Shutterstock; p. 3, chapter openers graphic (boxing ring) © www.istockphoto.com/Urs Siedentop.

Designer: Les Kanturek; Editor: Bethany Bryan; Photo Researcher: Marty Levick